Habitats and Wildlife in Danger

Sarah Levete

CRABTREE
Publishing Company
www.crabtreebooks.com

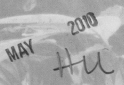

Crabtree Publishing Company
www.crabtreebooks.com

Author:
Sarah Lavete

Editorial director:
Kathy Middleton

Designer:
Paul Myerscough

Proofreaders:
Crystal Sikkens, Molly Aloian

Production coordinator:
Kenneth Wright

Prepress technician:
Kenneth Wright

Illustrations:
Geoff Ward

Cover:
War in the Congo has threatened mountain gorillas and their habitat.

Cover photograph:
Shutterstock (Renars Jurkovskis)

Photos:
Alamy Images: Jeff Greenberg p. 28; Corbis: Jonathan Blair p. 11, Reuters p. 13t, Isabelle Vayron/Sygma p. 26; Dreamstime: Bernard Breton p. 18, Agostino Celentano p. 21t, Forcdan p. 23t, Michael Mill p. 21b; Fotolia: Bartez p. 19t, Pix Harper p. 29t; Istockphoto: James Forte p. 9t, Nils Kahle p. 10; Joseph Luoman p. 16-17, 17b, Hougaard Malan p. 13b; Rex Features: Mark Brewer p. 14; Shutterstock: AKV p. 6-7, Kitch Bain p. 5, Paul Banton p. 27t, Bierchen p. 20-21, Vera Bogaerts p. 7b, Ian Bracegirdle p. 8-9, Ferenc Cegledi p. 25, FloridaStock p. 24, Daniel Gustavsson p. 24–25, Ifstewart p. 18–19, Andrejs Jegorovs p. 26–27, Gail Johnson p. 7t, 17t, LindyCro p. 15t, Christian Musat p. 12-13, Oksana Perkins p. 19b, Mikko Pitkänen p. 10–11, Dr. Morley Read p. 9b, Serg64 p. 28-29, Specta p. 22-23, Tania A p. 23b, Wong Yu Liang p. 1, 3, 14–15, 30–31, 32, A.S. Zain p. 4-5.

Library and Archives Canada Cataloguing in Publication
Levete, Sarah
        Habitats and wildlife in danger / Sarah Levete.

(Protecting our planet)
Includes index.
ISBN 978-0-7787-5213-4 (bound).--ISBN 978-0-7787-5230-1 (pbk.)

        1. Endangered species--Juvenile literature. 2. Endangered ecosystems--Juvenile literature. 3. Habitat conservation--Juvenile
literature. 4. Wildlife conservation--Juvenile literature.
5. Environmental degradation--Juvenile literature.
I. Title. II. Series: Protecting our planet (St. Catharines, Ont.)

QH75.L49 2010   j577.27   C2009-905232-6

Library of Congress Cataloging-in-Publication Data

Levete, Sarah.
  Habitats and wildlife in danger / Sarah Levete.
        p. cm. -- (Protecting our planet)
  Includes index.
ISBN 978-0-7787-5230-1 (pbk. : alk. paper) -- ISBN 978-0-7787-5213-4 (reinforced library binding : alk. paper)
1. Habitat conservation--Juvenile literature. 2. Wildlife conservation--Juvenile literature. 3. Endangered species--Juvenile literature. 4. Endangered ecosystems--Juvenile literature. I. Title. II. Series.

QH75.L44 2009
578.68--dc22

                                                                           2009034866

Crabtree Publishing Company

www.crabtreebooks.com   1-800-387-7650

Published in Canada
Crabtree Publishing
616 Welland Ave.
St. Catharines, ON
L2M 5V6

Published in the United States
Crabtree Publishing
PMB16A
350 Fifth Ave., 59th floor
New York, NY 10118

Printed in China/122009/CT20090915

Published by CRABTREE PUBLISHING COMPANY.
Copyright © **2010**

Contents

What are habitats?

Every animal has a place where it is most suited to living and breeding. These are habitats. Habitats change naturally, usually over a long time. For instance, a pond may become clogged up with plants. This affects the types of animals and plants that can thrive there.

A changing world

Human activity often changes natural habitats quickly. This means that animals and plants do not have time to adapt to the changes. Without a habitat, a species' existence is threatened. For instance, scientists believe that great apes could become **extinct** in the next 20 years as their natural habitat is being destroyed.

▼ *Habitat destruction in Borneo is the orangutan's greatest threat.*

"In the last 35 years about 50,000 orangutans are estimated to have been lost as their habitats shrank . . . The fate of the orangutan is a subject that goes to the heart of sustainable forests . . . To save the orangutan we have to save the forest."

Susilo Bambang Yudhoyono, President of Indonesia, December 2007

CASE STUDY

Orangutans under threat

You may not think that soap has anything to do with the destruction of the orangutan's home, but soap is often made from palm oil. This oil from palm trees is also used in many other items such as food, crayons, and candles. To produce this oil, huge areas of dense, tropical forest called rainforest are being replaced with palm trees.

Orangutans are losing their habitats. Their population is shrinking so much that their survival is under threat. One hundred years ago there were about 230,000 orangutans in Indonesia. Today there are only about 60,000.

Without dense forest, the tree-dwelling **primate** cannot survive. Orangutans climb through a canopy, which is a dense layer of rainforest trees, about 83 feet (30 meters), high. They sleep in nests, and feed mainly on fruit that grows on the trees. The rainforest habitat provides them with shelter, nests, and food. In return the orangutan helps to keep the forest fertile with a rich soil. Moving from branch to branch in the overhanging canopy, the orangutan opens up the cover of leaves and drops fruit and seeds to the ground. Sunlight

▲ *Orangutans live only on the Indonesian islands of Borneo and Sumatra.*

reaches the dark forest floor where the seeds are able to take root and grow into new trees for the rain forest.

In the orangutan's native islands of Indonesia, about 729,000 acres (1.8 million hectares) of rain forest are destroyed each year. With its unique habitat disappearing fast, we could lose the orangutan forever in just 15 years.

What makes a habitat?

From puddles to bushes, from streams to oceans, the planet is covered in different types of habitats. Large areas with similar weather patterns and vegetation, such as rain forests or deserts, are called **biomes**. There are smaller habitats within each biome. Earth's **biodiversity** is amazing. It is home to at least 13 billion animal and plant species.

Ecosystems

The word ecosystem is short for ecological system. An ecosystem includes every living thing in an area, and the things that affect their lives such as the weather and the soil. It is made up of many small communities interacting with each other. For example, in woodlands, decayed **fungi** enrich the soil in which trees and other plants grow. Fungi would not be able to survive without trees, dead leaf matter, and moisture. An ecosystem changes and develops over time.

Climate

The types of habitat and wildlife that survive and thrive in an area are influenced by **climate**. Frozen areas of land with little vegetation, called tundra, are found near the North Pole.

◄ *A damp forest floor provides the ideal habitat for fungi.*

▲ *The Arctic poppy is tough enough to be able to survive harsh Arctic winters.*

The weather here is very cold and the bare, freezing ground of the tundra supports low-growing plants such as mosses and lichen. These are plant-like organisms that grow on hard surfaces. These lie dormant, or sleeping, during the long, cold winter months.

Adaptation

Over millions of years, plants and animals have adapted to their habitat. For instance, a camel can survive with little water in extreme heat, but a woodland squirrel would soon die in the desert. The roots of many wetland plants, such as the bald cypress tree, are suited to a water-logged soil with little oxygen. Their roots above the soil take in oxygen from the air. Only a few plants can survive the harsh Arctic winters—the dwarf willow is covered in hairs to protect it from freezing.

Grasslands in temperate climates are often a riot of color in summer. ➤

Fact bank

Climate is determined by an area's latitude—its position relative to the **equator** where the Sun's rays are strongest. **Altitude** and distance from the ocean also influence the climate of an area. The main climate zones are:

• Desert: very low rainfall, usually with high daytime temperatures.

• Polar: very cold conditions, covered by snow and ice most of the year. Examples include the Arctic and the Antarctic.

• **Savannah**: one short rainy season followed by dry weather. Examples include Sahel in North Africa.

• Temperate: steady temperatures across the seasons. Examples include the United Kingdom. Canada and the United States have more extreme temperatures but are still included as temperate.

• Tropical: places near the equator; hot, wet and humid. Examples include the Amazon Basin.

Nature's balance

Habitats provide the **environment** in which animals and plants can thrive, supporting Earth's rich biodiversity. This biodiversity is the source of many foods, medicines, and breathtaking landscapes. Humans are interfering with the natural balance of Earth's ecosystems—with serious results.

Natural or unnatural change?

Habitats change due to natural causes and species become extinct. However, human activity is upsetting the natural balance of the environment. Clearing land to grow crops, and pollution from industry and farming, damages habitats and threatens the survival of wildlife.

The carbon cycle

Trees and plants release oxygen, which we breathe in. They also soak up a gas called carbon dioxide, acting as a sponge.

"Habitats the world over are under threat, with dire consequences for plant and animal species."

UNEP Global State of the Environment Report, 1997

Carbon dioxide helps control Earth's temperature by trapping in a certain amount of heat from the Sun. But too much carbon dioxide causes a worldwide rise in temperatures—global warming—as the gas traps too much heat around Earth. Burning fossil fuels such as coal and oil releases massive amounts of carbon dioxide. Burning trees also releases large amounts of the gas.

► *Huge amounts of fossil fuels are burned in electricity power stations. The waste gases produced by this contribute to global warming.*

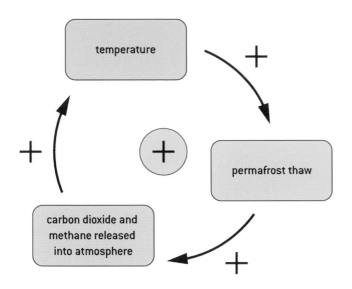

⋏ As temperatures rise, permanently frozen ground called permafrost begins to thaw. This releases greenhouse gases trapped within the frozen ground. This action causes a further rise in temperature.

Climate change

A major threat to habitats around the world is **climate change**. This is caused by the **greenhouse effect** of too much carbon dioxide and other greenhouse gases in the atmosphere. Climate change is warming up Earth's temperatures.

⋏ The rosy periwinkle is used to treat cancer. If Madagascan rain forests are destroyed, the flower could be lost forever.

This causes sea levels to rise, increasing the risk of flooding. There are more frequent extreme weather events such as severe storms and droughts, all of which have an impact on habitats.

▼ Habitats, such as the Amazon rain forest, are being destroyed. Many animals that live there, including the Amazon leaf frog, could vanish altogether.

Fact bank

• Forest destruction accounts for around 20 percent of greenhouse gas emissions.

• Every year 17 million acres (7 million hectares) of ancient forest are cleared or severely damaged—that's about 25 American football fields every minute!

9

Pushing animals aside

Advances in industry since the late 1800s have transformed the way humans live and the global population continues to increase. Everyone needs shelter, food, clean water, and access to technology. But modern advances have had a huge impact on habitats around the world. How can we balance the needs of humans with those of the natural world?

On the move

Highways allow us to easily get from one part of the country to another. But the roads cut through habitats. They also allow more cars to be on the road. This increases carbon dioxide emissions, which worsens climate change.

The land that airports are built on is also the home of animals. Airports, such as in Vancouver, Canada, try to manage the needs of the birds and the airport. Wildlife officers patrol the runways to divert the birds to a safer route. This is not always successful.

▼ *Even minor roads cause problems for wildlife such as deer.*

"Most of the world's endangered species—some 25 percent of mammals and 12 percent of birds—may become extinct over the next few decades as warmer conditions alter the forests, wetlands, and rangelands they depend on, and human development blocks them from migrating elsewhere."

"Feeling the Heat," UN Framework Convention on Climate Change, 2004

Coal

In India, coal mining is increasing to meet the growing population's need and demand for electricity produced by burning coal. The mines in the Jharkand region cut across areas of land once used as natural corridors for roaming tigers and elephants. These creatures used to cross from one isolated habitat to another along these forest routes. Without the corridors, the animals are deprived of their natural habitat and stray into villages, threatening the lives of local people.

▼ *Many airports have been built in areas in which wildlife live. This damages habitats and disturbs the animals that live there.*

WHAT CAN BE DONE?

Machines or explosives clear huge holes in the ground, called quarries, to get rocks, stones, and other materials used in buildings. Quarries can be left as ugly, gaping holes or filled with mounds of garbage, neither of which will encourage healthy new habitats for wildlife. However, the quarries can be restored to rich habitats such as wetlands. Planting seeds and plants that are suitable to the land type can encourage new growth. The new plants and trees become habitats for wildlife.

Farming pressures

It is estimated that Earth's population will increase by 3 billion by 2040. The pressure on farmers to produce more food as cheaply as possible is growing, too. This means farming on an **intensive** scale, and clearing large areas of land for crops. In many poor countries, farmers continuously grow crops in the same fields, which takes all the **nutrients** out of the soil.

Buzzing off

The sight of a buzzing bumblebee landing on a flower is becoming less common. The bee population is in decline. Scientists believe that this is connected to their loss of habitat as fields are cleared for growing crops and for building new homes. Bees are pollinators, transferring pollen from plant to plant—some scientists say that every third mouthful we eat is the result of bee pollination!

Crops for fuel

The demand for cheaper and more environmentally friendly alternative energy sources has led to a massive rise in the growth of crops for **biofuels**, which do not release locked-up carbon dioxide in the same way as fossil fuels.

◄ *Pesticides and other harmful chemicals used in modern farming can seep into the water and kill fish in many rivers.*

Farmers clear land to grow crops, such as corn, palm, and rapeseed, which can be turned into biofuels. These soak up carbon dioxide as they grow, which balances out the amount of carbon dioxide released when they are burned. However, large amounts of carbon dioxide are released when forests are burned to clear the land to grow the crops. Many people also believe that the land used for growing biofuel crops should be used to grow food for the increasing population.

▲ *Fish poisoned by chemicals in polluted rivers cannot be eaten by people.*

CASE STUDY

English hedgerows

Rows of hedges crisscross the English landscape, providing boundaries between fields as well as crucial habitats for butterflies, moths, birds, and small mammals. However, between 1950 and 1998 thousands of miles (km) of hedgerows were cut down every year to make way for larger fields, roads, and building land. Since then, new laws in England now require farmers to apply for special permission to remove a hedgerow. Many farmers have even replanted hedgerows on their land.

Growing Algae

Farmers often use artificial chemicals to keep crops free of pests and to make them grow as fast as possible. The chemicals also destroy weeds or wildflowers that are habitats for many creatures. Chemicals seep into the soil, and often run off into rivers and lakes. This causes tiny plants called algae to grow. The algae choke the water and use up so much oxygen from it that there is not enough to support other plant and fish life.

This field has been sprayed with chemicals and supports little wildlife. The hedgerows have been ripped out. ➤

The cost of war

Since World War II there have been hundreds of wars. Some have involved several countries. Others have been civil wars between groups in the same country. War refugees settle wherever they can, often on land which cannot support larger populations. The effects of war on animal and plant habitats can be devastating.

Burning up

During the Gulf War in 1991, Iraqi soldiers set light to more than 500 oil wells in Kuwait. They also dumped thousands of tons of oil into the Persian Gulf. Thick black smoke covered the area for months. Pollution in the air poisoned vegetation and animals for miles around. More than 25,000 birds were destroyed in the spills of thick oil. The full impact on the environment has yet to be assessed.

Landmines

There are over 40 million landmines in the ground in over 70 countries. Landmines are weapons hidden in the ground which explode when someone walks or drives over them. When a landmine explodes, the mine kills and maims people nearby. Mines also have a serious environmental impact. As the landmine casings explode, poisons seep out into the ground. These can affect the long-term health of the surrounding soil and harm water supplies.

◀ *Burning oil wells in Kuwait caused huge damage to the environment.*

14

▲ *War in the Congo has threatened the mountain gorillas that live there.*

Breakdown

During a war, usual organizations are unable to work. Conservation efforts, or looking after the natural environment, are no longer a priority. There are about 700 mountain gorillas left in the world. About 100 of these are in the Virunga Park in the Congo. Conflict in the area has forced park rangers to flee and they no longer protect the gorillas.

▼ *Warfare can destroy ecosystems and threaten huge areas of habitat.*

CASE STUDY

Agent Orange

The Americans were active in the Vietnam War, fighting North Vietnam, from 1965 to 1973. The American military wanted to clear the thick forest so that they could spot North Vietnamese soldiers more easily and prevent them from ambushing American soldiers. Using helicopters, the Americans sprayed 19 million gallons (72 million liters) of chemicals onto the lush vegetation below. The most famous of these was code named Agent Orange after the color of the **herbicide's** container. During the war, 3.2 million acres (1.3 million hectares) of forest were destroyed, wiping out natural habitats and destroying ecosystems.

Rain forests in danger

From hot and steamy tropical rain forests to cooler temperate forests in North America, forests are like the lungs of the world—they keep Earth supplied with a healthy balance of oxygen and carbon dioxide.

Why cut them down?

Rain forests are burned or felled to clear the land to grow crops, including biofuels. Timber, such as mahogany and teak, is taken from felled trees and sold across the world for use in items such as furniture.

A long history—a quick death

More than 50 percent of Earth's plant and animal species live in tropical rain forests. With towering trees and colorful birds, twists of climbing plants and hanging creatures, carpets of forest floors crawling with insects, and deep swirling rivers—these are Earth's richest and most diverse habitats. One 3.86 square-mile (10 square-km) area contains about 1,500 species of flowering plants! On the island of Madagascar, off the eastern coast of Africa, over three-quarters of the plants and animals are found nowhere else on Earth.

◄ *Cutting down rain forest trees threatens the habitats and the survival of thousands of species of insects and plants.*

▲ *Madagascar is home to many unique plant and animal species, including these lemurs.*

However, many lemurs, such as the aye-aye and the golden-crowned sifaka, are now endangered species. Madagascar's tropical rainforest habitat is under threat. Without it, countless species of plants and animals will not survive. The destruction of a rain forest wipes out ancient and unique living things.

Soil and sky

When leaves fall from the trees, their nutrients are used up again by other plants and trees. Clearing a rain forest of its native trees affects the soil's composition, or makeup. Without covers of leaves, the soil dries up quickly in the sun and without plants to hold the water in the soil, it just washes away in the rain. The remaining soil is weak and is often unable to support any growth. In time, it can turn to desert. Tropical rain forests help regulate Earth's climate as they soak up huge amounts of carbon dioxide and keep global temperatures in balance. Much of the moisture stored in rain forest vegetation evaporates back into the atmosphere as rainfall—without this, droughts around the world are more likely.

WHAT CAN BE DONE?

The South American country Guyana is covered with rain forest. Scientists estimate that 2.5 million acres (1 million hectares) of forest contain 118 million tons (120 million tonnes) of carbon—that's about the same amount as annual carbon emissions in the United Kingdom! Guyana's government has rented a million hectares of forest to the British government. While the British government protects this habitat, Guyana receives much-needed income. This then helps the invaluable rain forest to survive.

▼ *Huge areas of rain forests are being destroyed in Brazil to make way for farming land.*

17

Polar perils

The bleak, icy white Arctic regions around the North Pole and tundra areas are surprisingly rich in wildlife. These freezing cold habitats have a range of dwarf plants, mosses, and animals such as the polar bear and reindeer. But global warming is melting the chilly habitats around both poles, threatening the survival of some species.

South Pole

The coastal areas of the Antarctic near the South Pole are habitats for penguins. Thick sea ice is the nesting ground for some penguins. If the ice is too thin and breaks up too soon, the chicks are swept to sea before they are ready to take care of themselves. The decrease in sea ice has reduced the amount of shrimp-like creatures called krill, and fish, which are the main food sources for penguins.

Meltdown

The consequences of global warming are serious both for the animals that live around the poles—and for humans around the rest of the world. Ice reflects heat back to the Sun. Without layers of ice, more heat will be absorbed into Earth's atmosphere, raising temperatures around the world even more. If all the ice in the Arctic and Antarctic melted, the meltwater would raise sea levels by at least another 39 feet (12 m) worldwide, flooding vast areas of coastland and many cities.

◄ *Emperor penguins are under threat as the ice melts in Antarctica. If the ice shrinks, so does their habitat.*

CASE STUDY

Threat to reindeer

Animals affected by the Arctic's changing climate include reindeer. These animals dig through ice to graze on lichen and moss. However, increasingly heavy rain falls onto the Arctic snow and seeps into the soil where it freezes. This thick layer of ice is too hard for the reindeer to break through. Reindeer migrate between their breeding and grazing grounds. Warmer temperatures caused by climate change are melting the permafrost and breaking the ice,

▲ *Reindeer feast on the mosses and lichen in the Arctic tundra.*

making the reindeers' route much more treacherous. An additional threat to the reindeers' survival is the building of roads and laying of pipes to carry supplies of oil.

A delicate balance

Animals, such as the Arctic fox, survive the extreme temperatures and conditions of the tundra. But the ecosystem is delicately balanced and very fragile. If the population of one species declines, it has a direct effect on another.

For instance, if there are not enough plants for lemmings and voles to eat and their numbers decrease, then the Arctic fox, a predator or hunter of lemmings and voles, is also at risk.

◄ *This lake is found in an area of northern Canada that lies within the Arctic circle. It is an example of the varied habitats found in the Arctic region.*

19

Sea and shores in crisis

The vast swirling oceans are Earth's largest ecosystem. From the warm surface waters dappled with sunlight to the icy depths thousands of yards (meters) below, the oceans are habitats to a vast range of animal and plant life. Rugged rocks, sandy shores, wavy sand dunes—the coastlines where land meets sea are also habitats for sea creatures, land animals, and birds.

Reshaping the land

For millions of years, waves and winds have lashed the land, helping to form dramatic coastlines, the boundary between land and sea. This natural erosion shapes the coastline. However, human activity is throwing coastlines into crisis. Building vacation resorts along the coast disrupts the landscape's natural defenses against storms and waves. Coastal areas are much more vulnerable to flooding. More extreme storms such as hurricanes, as well as rising sea levels caused by warmer temperatures increase the risk of flooding coastlines.

> "Entire ecosystems in the high seas are being damaged and lost before we have even acted to protect them."
>
> **Closing statement, IUCN Marine Protected Area Summit, April 2007**

◄ *The sea and its shores are home to thousands of animal species, some of which we may have not yet discovered.*

Fishing to death

Certain fishing practices threaten some ocean habitats. Huge trawlers drag heavy nets along the sea floor, smashing everything in their path. Catching too many fish before they can naturally reproduce reduces the population of some fish, such as cod in the North Atlantic. Dolphins, which share habitats with tuna, often become caught in nets designed to catch tuna.

▲ *Coastal developments are a threat to manatees and their diet of sea-grass.*

Litter kills

A discarded plastic bag or water bottle left on the beach after a picnic looks unattractive, but it is also deadly to creatures that live on the shore. A sea creature may swallow the bag, believing it to be food, and the bag then causes it to suffocate. Dumping litter in the sea does not safely or effectively get rid of garbage. A foam cup can take 80 years to degrade or rot away. An aluminum pull-tab takes 200 years.

Birds

Warmer waters and rising sea levels caused by climate change affect birds along the coast. Shorebirds around the world depend on mudflats and beaches in order to feed and nest. With sea levels rising, many shorebirds will lose their breeding and nesting grounds and their **migration** routes—their populations will decline.

WHAT CAN BE DONE?

Many countries around the world have established special marine reserves in order to protect certain fish and seafood species from overfishing. Some countries have banned the sale of tuna unless it has been caught in a dolphin-friendly way—that is without killing dolphins in the fishing nets when catching the tuna.

Wading birds, such as sandpipers, often spend their winters along the coast. ►

21

Crumbling coral reefs

Coral reefs are sometimes called the rainforests of the sea. Like tropical rainforests, they are habitats to thousands of species of plants and animals. Coral reefs are built by groups of polyps, small creatures that leave behind a hard skeleton. The skeletons build up over hundreds of years, slowly forming a complex, delicate structure called a coral reef.

Turning white

Strange plant-animals called zooxanthellae provide the coral polyp with food, taken from the Sun's energy through **photosynthesis**. The effects of pollution and warming seas kill the zooxanthellae, depriving the coral of food. The color drains out of the coral, causing it to bleach, or turn white. Some corals cannot survive the effect of bleaching.

"Ocean chemistry is changing to a state that has not occurred for hundreds of thousands of years . . . Shell-building by marine organisms will slow down or stop. Reef-building will decrease or reverse."

Richard Feely of Seattle's Pacific Marine Environmental Laboratory, February 2007

◄ *Coral reefs are an important habitat, supporting many marine species.*

◄ *Atolls are coral islands consisting of a reef surrounding a lagoon.*

they can easily be caught damages the delicate coral. Overfishing threatens the reef's natural biodiversity. If too many plant-eating fish are caught, the reef may become overrun with plants which block out sunlight and prevent healthy growth of the polyps.

Blasted and broken

Coral reefs provide humans with a diverse supply of fish to eat. But some fishing methods are destroying the fishes' habitat. Blasting dynamite near a reef to bring fish to the surface where

Impact of losing reefs

Since 1998, 16 percent of all tropical reefs have been lost due to the effects of bleaching, warmer seas, pollution, and some fishing practices. By 2050 it is thought they could disappear altogether. A billion people will suffer, as they rely on fish for protein in their diets, and a beautiful habitat will be destroyed. Coral reefs also protect the coastline from the effects of surging storms and winds. Without them, rising seas will reach further inland, flooding coastal habitats, too.

Fact bank

The Great Barrier Reef in Australia covers 135,000 square miles (349,000 square km). It is habitat to:

- Nearly 8 percent (1,500) of Earth's fish species.

- Over 700 species of coral.

- Over 4,000 species of mollusks.

- Over 250 species of birds, which nest and breed there.

- Five species of turtles.

Fishing methods that preserve the beautiful coral reefs should be used at all times to protect this rich habitat. ►

Wetlands under threat

Wetlands are areas of land filled or soaked with water. They include lakes, bogs, and marshes. In some wetlands, giant grasses grow up to 9 feet (3 m) high and there are floating meadows of plants, such as the papyrus.

A watery home

Wetlands are home to plants that have adapted to wet conditions. These areas are important sources of fresh water, help protect the land from wind and storms, and are habitats to many animal and plant species. However, human activity endangers wetlands. Building on wetlands, the effect of pollution, and poor management of the land threatens these rich habitats.

Salty trees

Trees called mangroves form forests by tropical seashores. The twisted mangrove roots grow above ground, and trap mud and sediment. Many mangrove forests have been cut back to make way for "fish farms" where fish are farmed and sold in large numbers. However, without the protection of twisting mangrove trees to soak up water from the seas and to act as a buffer against fierce winds, storms and hurricanes batter the coastline more quickly and flood the land.

◄ *The Everglades ecosystem in Florida provides a home to more than 350 species of birds.*

24

Dried up

A 33-mile (53-km) sea wall built in South Korea to drain the Saemangeum wetlands threatens the survival of birds such as the Nordmann's greenshank and spoonbilled sandpiper. The area was meant for rice-growing, but a lack of fresh water prevented this. The wall remains, and the land is dry. The birds have lost a feeding and resting ground on their lengthy journey as they migrate from cold climates to warmer ones.

▼ *Once an endangered species, the American alligator is now legally protected.*

WHAT CAN BE DONE?

The Ramsar Convention represents a response to the threat over wetland habitats. In 1971, scientists and officials from many countries met in the Iranian city of Ramsar to discuss how they could protect the future of these habitats and areas. The countries that signed up to the agreement agreed to select one wetland every year which they would protect.

The first wetland site protected by the United States was the Everglades in Florida. Habitat to the Florida panther, manatee, southern bald eagle, and alligator, the wetland has suffered from the effects of pollution and diverting water from its natural river courses.

Grassy habitats

Grasslands are areas dominated by various kinds of grasses, and have few or no trees. They make up one-quarter of Earth's land. Grasslands are divided into two types: temperate grasslands and tropical grasslands, called savannahs. Both are home to many grazing and roaming animals.

Threats

Poaching or illegal hunting, overgrazing, and clearing land for crops are the main threats to grasslands. About 16 percent of tropical grasslands have been converted for agriculture or urban development. Much of the temperate grasslands have been turned into farms or grazing land. This is because the area is flat, treeless, covered with grass, and has rich soil. Ploughing up grasslands for agriculture and pasture has also destroyed habitats for insects, including pollinators. Birds have been left without grasses, grains, and insects to eat. There is no food left for grazing animals or their predators.

Grassy lands

Both tropical savannahs and temperate grasslands are rich habitats for wild flowers, insects, birds, and animals. Grass, the dominant plant in these habitats, is very important. Migrating geese making the long journey from Scotland to Greenland need a lot of energy and rely on the grasslands to provide this. Huge herds of saiga antelope once roamed the steppes—vast grassy plains in Russia and Asia—which now have been turned mostly into farmland.

Australian farmers and cattle ranchers could improve the soil of their overfarmed grasslands by replanting grasses there. ➤

Land of elephants

Over half of Africa is covered in savannah. Savannahs have dry and rainy seasons. They range from open woodland to huge grassy areas. The West Sudanian savannah is a dry, woody habitat.

▲ *Giraffes rely on a diet of thorny plants that grow in their grassy savannah habitat.*

CASE STUDY

Prairie dogs

Elaborate burrows and underground chambers with separate living and eating areas were once common across the Great Plains from southern Canada to northern Mexico. These were the homes of the black-tailed prairie dog. The changing face of their habitat as the grasslands are turned into crop-growing fields has caused a dramatic decline in the number of prairie dogs. These habitats have also provided homes for snakes and burrowing owls.

A growing human population has increased pressure on the land, parts of which are overfarmed. With drier conditions due to climate change, the soil often takes a long time to recover its fertility. The poaching of large mammals is a problem, and elephants have reduced greatly in number. Savannah elephants push over trees and shrubs and eat them, making space for grass to grow. With fewer elephants, more shrubs remain and grass cannot grow. Antelope numbers have declined due to the reduction in grass, so there is less prey for lions.

▼ *The loss of savannah grassland in Africa is threatening the big cat population there.*

27

Protecting our planet

Without habitats, there is no wildlife. With damaged habitats wildlife suffers, species are wiped out, and ecosystems destroyed. Human activity is greatly responsible for the accelerating rate at which natural habitats are in decline. Awareness of the problem enables us to take action—before it is too late.

Working hard

Conservation groups work to preserve habitats. In the United Kingdom, for example, only a small amount of ancient woodland remains, much of which exists in small, isolated pockets. The **Forestry Commission** is working to set up "habitat networks" that allow plants and animals to move in response to changing climates and conditions. A computer system provides digital maps of forests. These show where it would be most effective to plant new woodland, so that animals, such as squirrels, could move across the intervening space in response to climate change.

◄ *Once a pond is cleared, new plant species will arrive, along with birds and mammals.*

We can all get involved in helping to protect different habitats and their wildlife.

- On vacation, do not buy souvenirs taken from nature, such as coral ornaments.

- Visit local nature reserves, national parks, and wildlife projects near your home and while on vacation. Your support can help them survive.

- Save up to help international habitat protection schemes. Through some of these, you might be able to buy your very own piece of rain forest or other wild place.

- Garbage can kill. Do not leave any litter in the countryside or on the beach.

- Offer to help clean-ups of local ponds, parks, canals, or seashores.

- Grow wild flowers in your garden or in a window box.

▲ *Even in a built-up city, gardens can be developed and cultivated.*

- When you are out walking, avoid treading on soil where wild flowers are growing. This flattens the soil, making it harder for the young seedlings to push through the earth.

- Whether you live in a busy city or a remote countryside area, find out about your local environment and the natural species that live there.

- Find out which local birds are under threat. Provide drinking water and the right foods to attract them.

▼ *Look after your own local ponds and wildlife havens.*

Glossary

altitude The height above sea level

biodiversity The variety of all living things

biofuel A fuel made from plants

biome A large area, such as a desert, with a characteristic climate and vegetation

climate The average weather in an area over a period of time

climate change Changes in Earth's weather patterns caused by human activity

endangered At risk of becoming extinct

environment The surroundings of plants, animals, and humans, from the soil to the weather

equator An imaginary line that circles the middle of Earth

extinct Not existing any more

Forestry Commission Government department in the United Kingdom responsible for the protection of forests and woodlands

fungi (singular, fungus) Plant-like organisms, such as toadstools and mushrooms, that grow on plants or on decayed material

greenhouse effect The warming effect of gases, such as carbon dioxide, which trap the Sun's heat around Earth

herbicide A chemical that destroys plants, used to control weeds

intensive Of farming, mass-producing food (plants and animals) by the use of chemical fertilizers, additives, and pesticides

migration Traveling back and forward on a seasonal basis. Animals, especially birds, migrate from one area to another, and back again for feeding and breeding

nutrients Goodness found in soil

photosynthesis The process by which green plants produce nutrients for growth from carbon dioxide and water, using sunlight. The process also produces oxygen

primate The order of mammals that includes humans, monkeys, and apes

savannah Open areas of grassland

sustainable Resources or habitats that are managed and used in a way that protects their long-term future

Further information

Books

*John Muir: Protecting and Preserving the Environment
(Voices for Green Choices),* Henry Elliott (Crabtree, 2009)

Environments (Sustainable World), Rob Bowden (Wayland, 2007)

Around the Poles (Habitats), Robert Snedden (Franklin Watts, 2004)

Tropical Grasslands (Habitats), Robert Snedden (Franklin Watts, 2004)

Tropical Rainforests (Habitats), Robert Snedden (Franklin Watts, 2004)

Web sites

Find out about different biomes around the world:

www.mbgnet.net/sets/index.htm

Take a look at this fun Web site for children run by Defenders of
Wildlife with fact sheets on many habitats and wildlife:

www.kidsplanet.org

Find out more on a wide range of environmental issues from
the WWF children's Web site at:

www.panda.org/who_we_are/wwf_offices/usa
www.panda.org/who_we_are/wwf_offices/canada

The Web site from Friends of the Earth has a lot of information about
the impact of climate change on wildlife and habitats:

www.foe.org/
www.foecanada.org/

Index